PIANO / VOCAL / GUITAR

THE BEST OF MATT REDMAN

ISBN 978-1-4234-8406-6

HAL•LEONARD®
CORPORATION

7777 W. BLUEMOUND RD. P.O. BOX 13819 MILWAUKEE, WI 53213

Visit Hal Leonard Online at
www.halleonard.com

BEAUTIFUL NEWS

Words and Music by
MATT REDMAN

With a strong beat

Joy is the theme of my song and the beat of my heart, and that joy is found __ in You. _ For You showed the pow'r of Your cross and Your great sav-ing love, and my soul woke up ____ to You. _

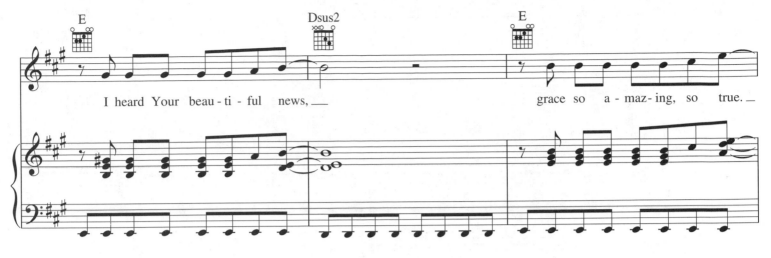

D.S. al Coda

cel - e - brate Your beau - ti - ful news.

CODA

cel - e - brate Your beau - ti - ful news. ___

There's a God who came down ___ to ___ save, ___

yeah. _ Showed the world His a - maz -

- ing __ grace. __ Did you know? __

There's a God who came down __ to __ save, __ and __

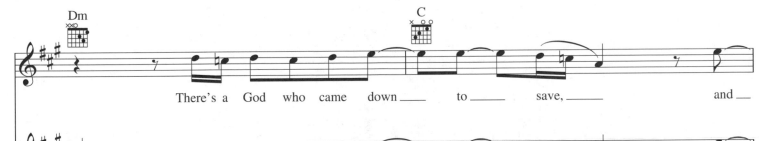

__ He calls __ Your name. __

-er still.__ Sav - ior, we're sing-ing now to cel - e - brate Your beau-ti-ful news,__

to

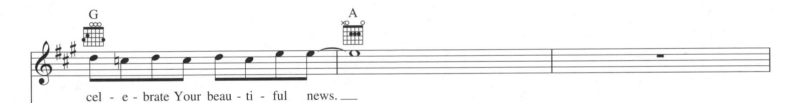

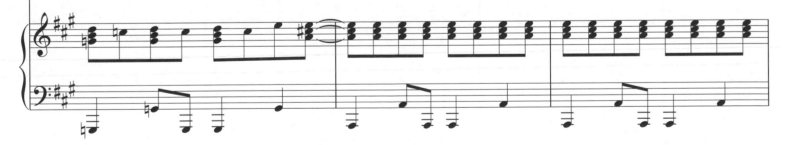

cel - e - brate Your beau - ti - ful news.__

Beau - ti - ful __ news. __

BETTER IS ONE DAY

Words and Music by
MATT REDMAN

Driving

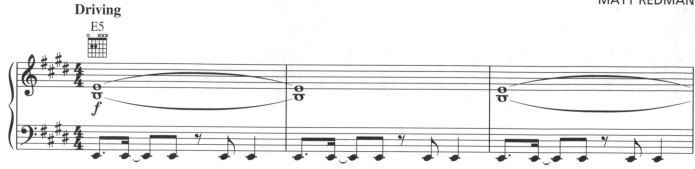

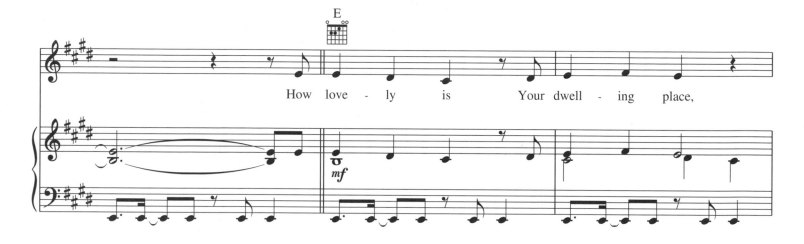

How love-ly is Your dwell-ing place,

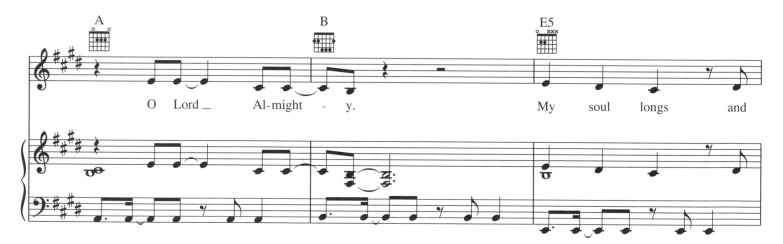

O Lord __ Al-might - y.   My soul longs and

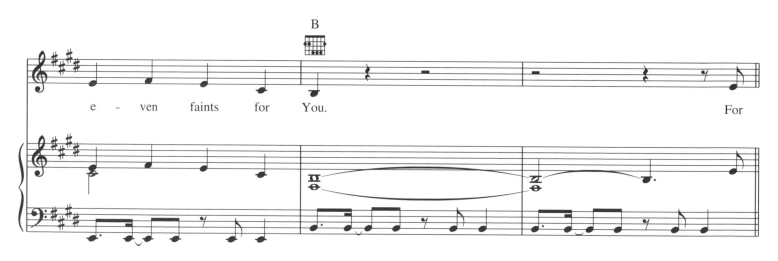

e - ven faints for You.   For

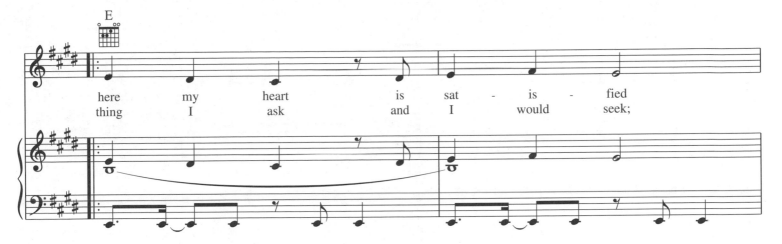

here my heart is sat - is - fied
thing I ask and I would seek;

with - in _____ Your pres - ence, I
to see _____ Your beau - ty, to

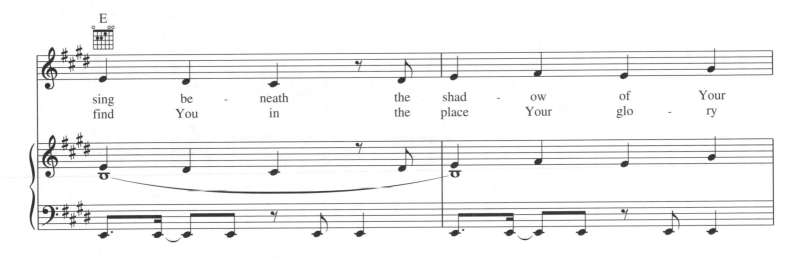

sing be - neath the shad - ow of Your
find You in the place Your of glo - ry

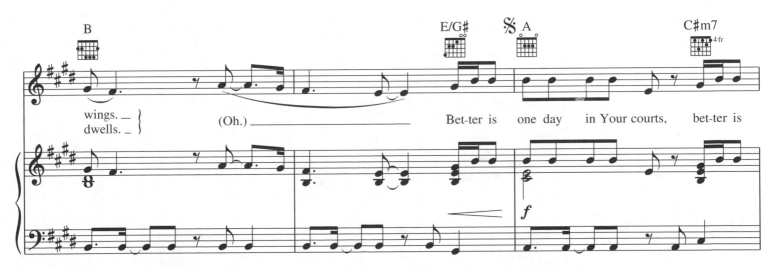

wings. _ } (Oh.) _____ Bet-ter is one day in Your courts, bet-ter is
dwells. _ }

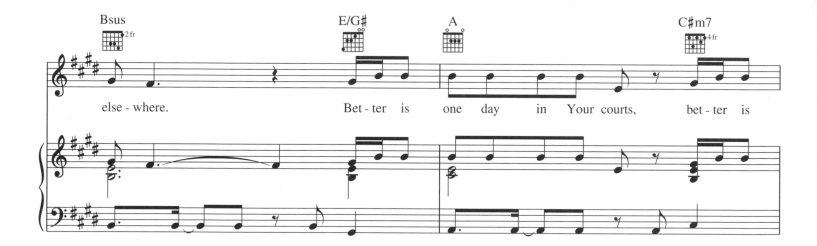

One else-where. Bet-ter is

else - where. _ My heart and flesh cry out for You, the liv-ing God. _

Your Spir-it's wa-ter for my soul. I've tast-ed and I've seen,

come once a-gain to me; _ I will draw near to You, _ I will draw near to You, _

to You.

(Draw near to You.)

(I will draw

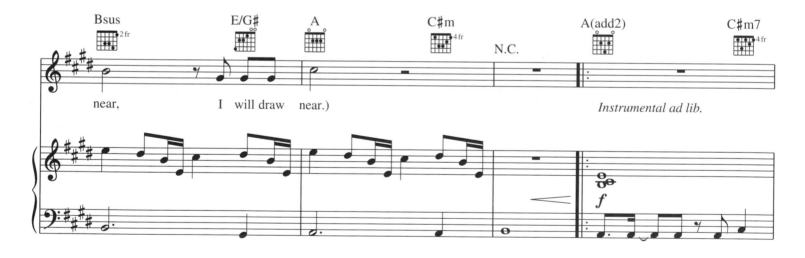

near, I will draw near.)

Instrumental ad lib.

Repeat and Fade **Optional Ending**

BLESSED BE YOUR NAME

Words and Music by MATT REDMAN
and BETH REDMAN

*Recorded a half step lower.

be Your name.
be Your name.

Bless - ed   be _____ Your name _____   when I'm
Bless - ed   be _____ Your name _____   on the

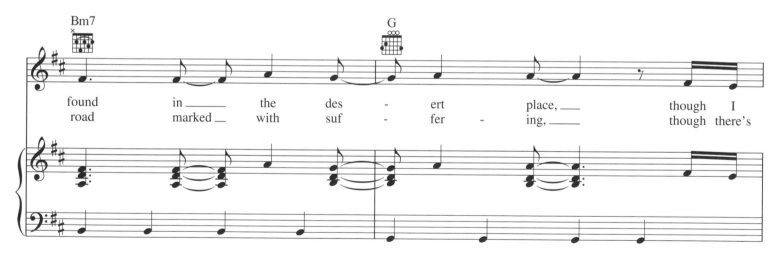

found   in _____ the des - ert place, _____ though I
road   marked __ with suf - fer - ing, _____ though there's

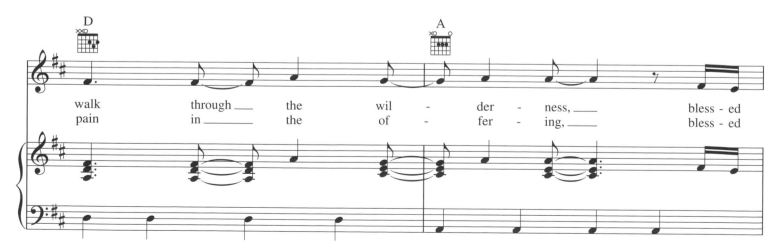

walk   through _____ the wil - der - ness, _____ bless - ed
pain   in _____ the of - fer - ing, _____ bless - ed

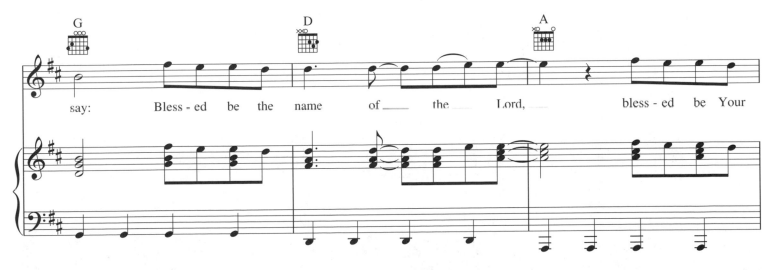

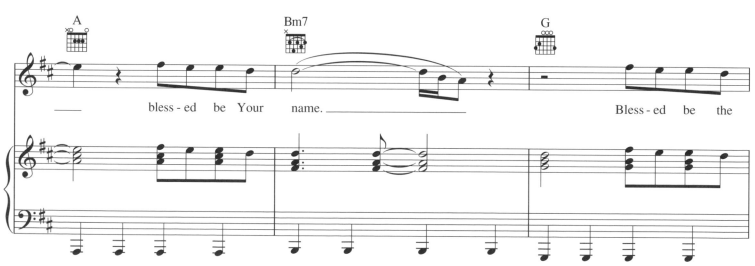

DANCING GENERATION

Words and Music by
MATT REDMAN

With excitement

Your mer - cy taught us

how to dance, __ to cel - e - brate with all we have, __ and __ we'll

dance _____ to thank _____ You for mer - cy.

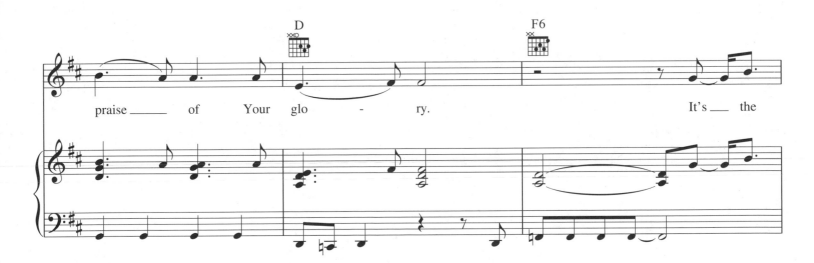

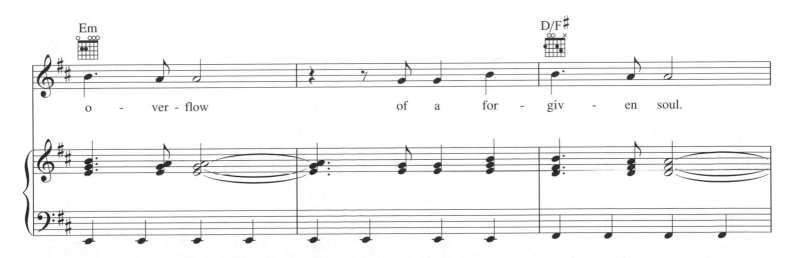

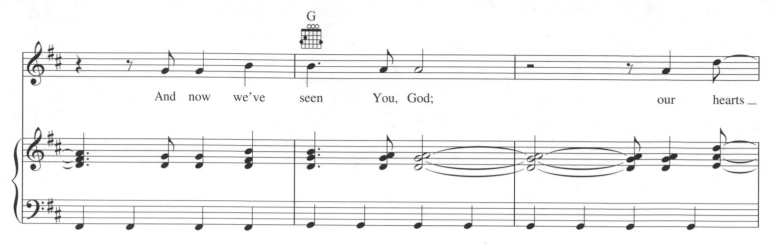

And now we've seen You, God; our hearts

can - not stay si - lent. And we'll be a danc - ing

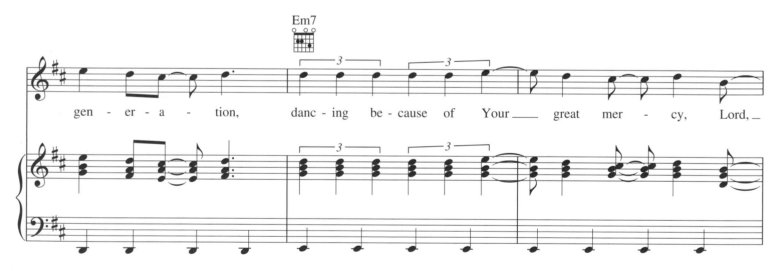

gen - er - a - tion, danc - ing be - cause of Your ___ great mer - cy, Lord, ___

Your ___ great mer - cy, Lord. ___

24

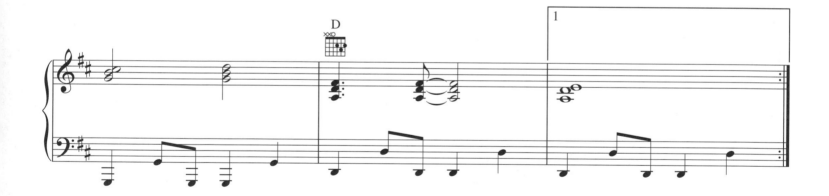

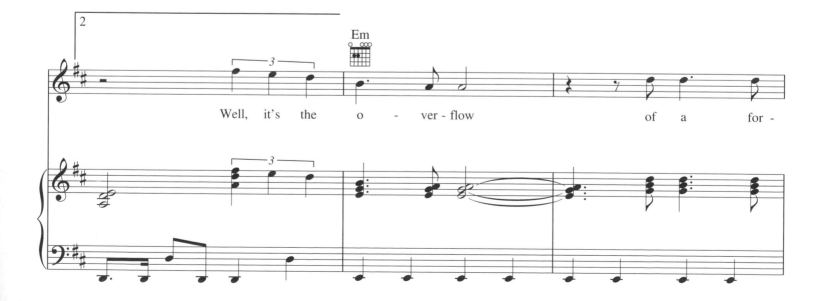

Well, it's the o - ver - flow   of a for -

giv - en soul. _____ And now we've seen You, God;

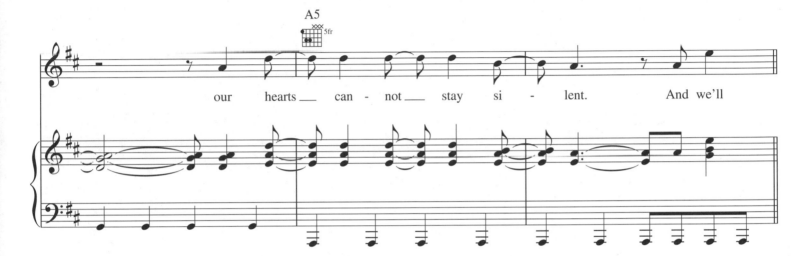

our hearts __ can - not __ stay si - lent. And we'll

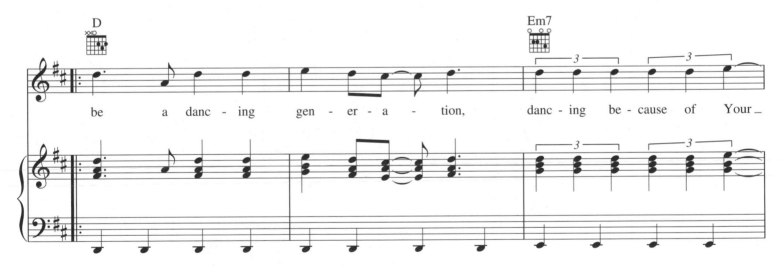

be a danc - ing gen - er - a - tion, danc - ing be - cause of Your __

__ great mer - cy, Lord, __ Your __ great mer - cy, Lord. __

Yes, we'll be a shout-ing

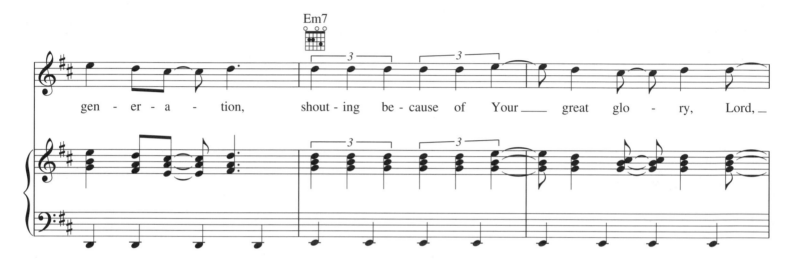

gen - er - a - tion, shout-ing be - cause of Your ___ great glo - ry, Lord, ___

Your ___ great glo - ry, Lord. ___

And we'll

Lord!

THE HEART OF WORSHIP

Words and Music by
MATT REDMAN

all a-bout You, __ all a-bout You, __ Je - sus. I'm sor - ry, Lord, for the thing __

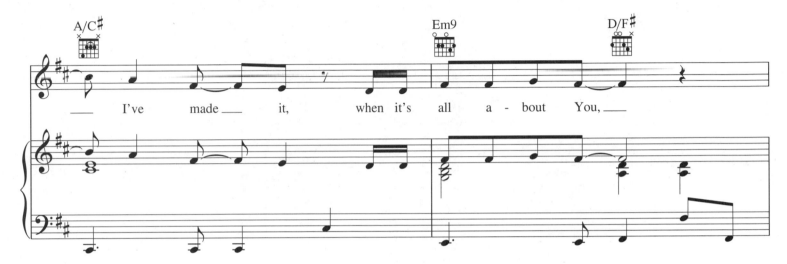

__ I've made __ it, when it's all a - bout You, __

all a-bout You, __ Je - sus. __

FACEDOWN

Words and Music by MATT REDMAN
and BETH REDMAN

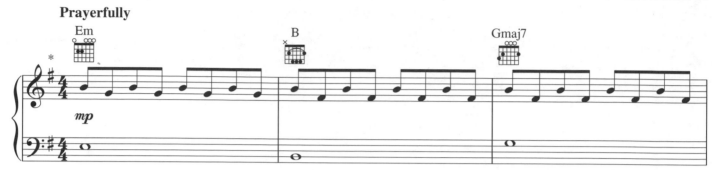

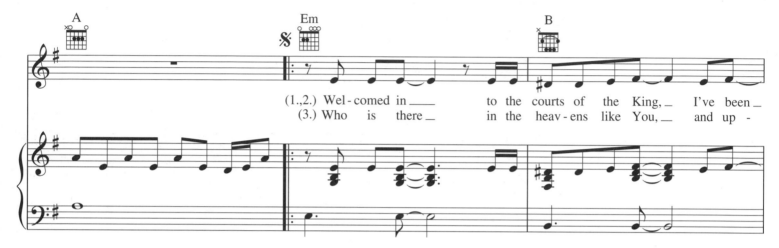

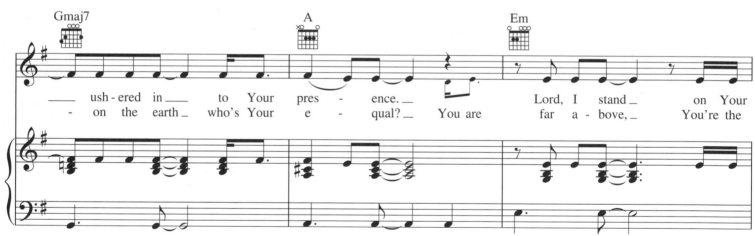

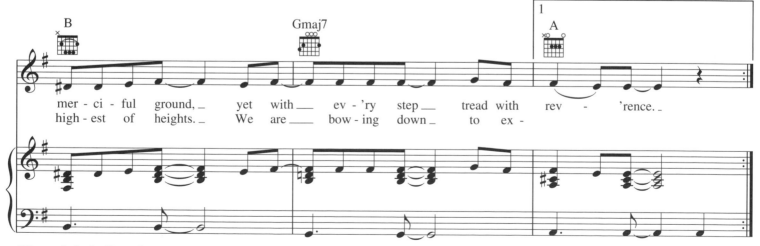

*Recorded a half step lower.

rev - 'rence. ___
alt ___ You. ___

And I'll

fall face-down as Your glo - ry shines a - round. ___

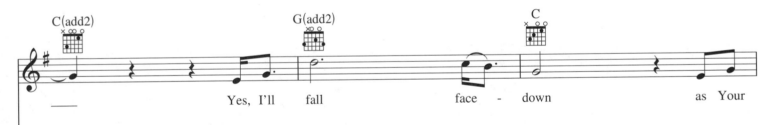

Yes, I'll fall face-down as Your

D.S. al Coda
(take 2nd ending)

To Coda

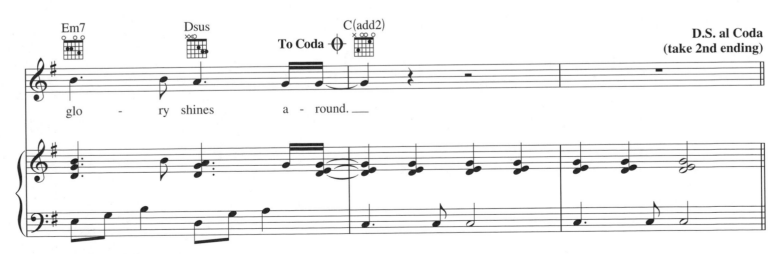

glo - ry shines a - round. ___

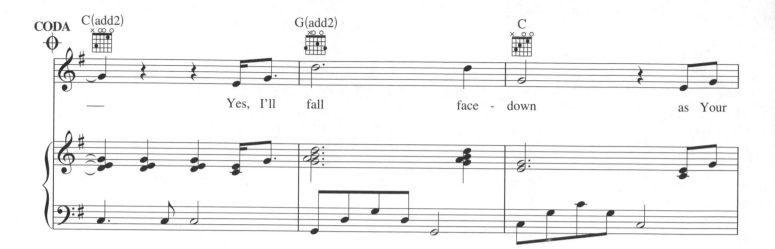

Yes, I'll fall face-down as Your

glo-ry shines a-round. ___ God, I'll fall face-

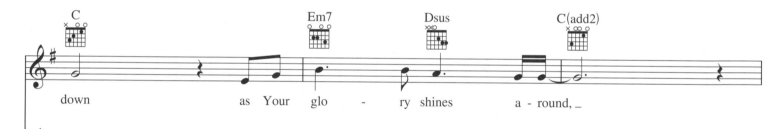

down as Your glo-ry shines a-round, __

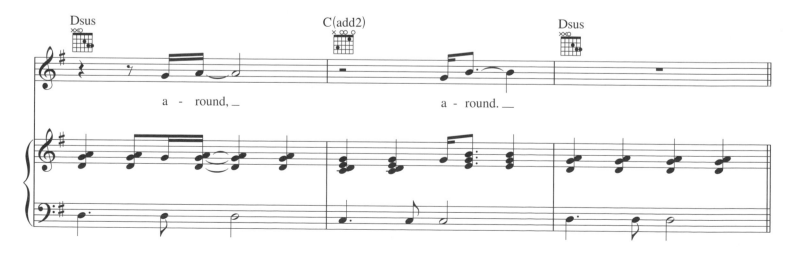

a-round, __ a-round. __

So let Your glo-ry shine a-round, __ let Your glo-ry shine a-round. King of glo-ry, here be

found, __ King of glo-ry. found, __ King of glo-ry. So let Your glo-ry shine a-

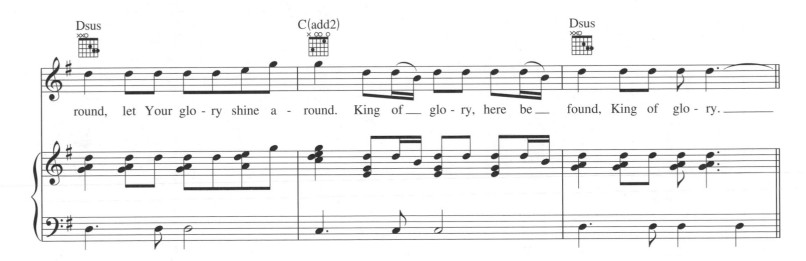

round, let Your glo-ry shine a-round. King of __ glo-ry, here be __ found, King of glo-ry. ____

(Vocal 1st time only)

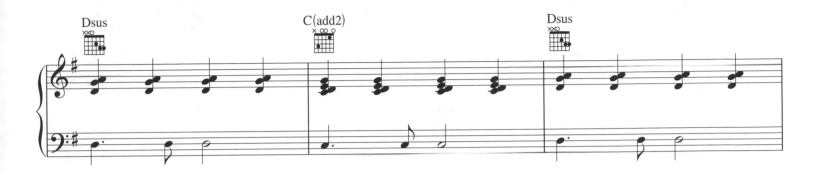

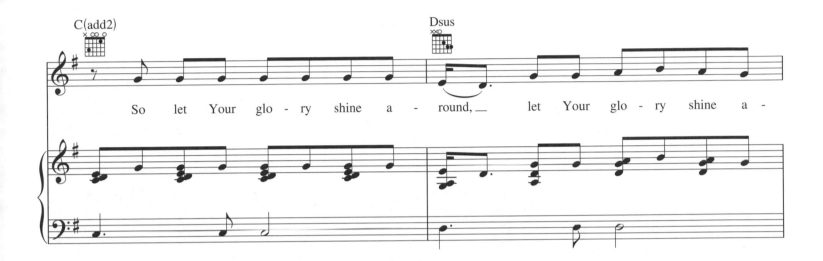

So let Your glo-ry shine a - round, __ let Your glo - ry shine a -

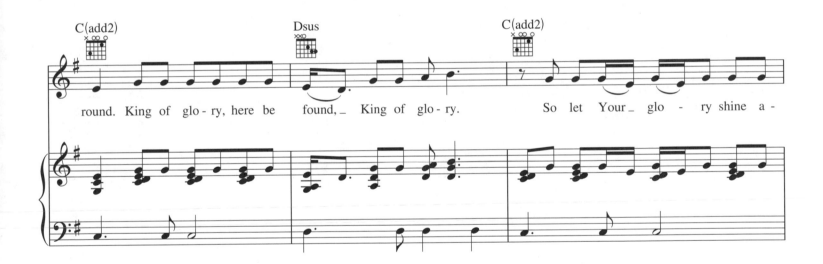

round. King of glory, here be found, __ King of glo - ry. So let Your __ glo - ry shine a -

round, __ let Your glo - ry __ shine a - round. King of glory, here be found, __ King of glo - ry.

LET EVERYTHING THAT HAS BREATH

Words and Music by
MATT REDMAN

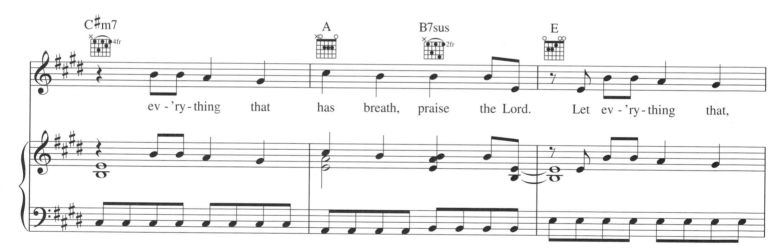

Let ev-'ry-thing that, ev-'ry-thing that,

ev-'ry-thing that has breath, praise the Lord. Let ev-'ry-thing that,

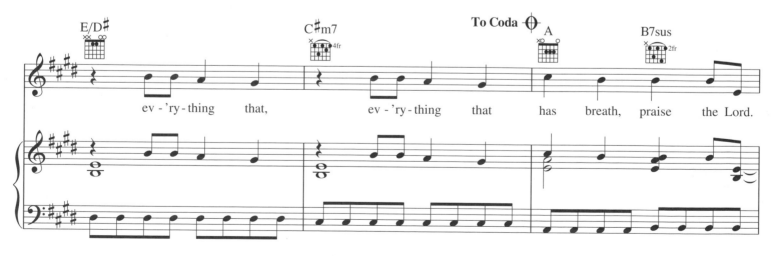

ev-'ry-thing that, ev-'ry-thing that has breath, praise the Lord.

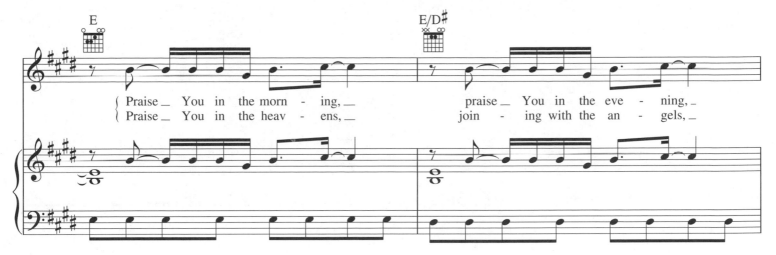

Praise __ You in the morn - ing, __ praise __ You in the eve - ning, __
Praise __ You in the heav - ens, __ join - ing with the an - gels, __

praise __ You when I'm young and when I'm old.
prais - ing You for - ev - er and a day.

Praise __ You when I'm laugh - ing, __ praise __ You when I'm griev - ing, __
Praise __ You on the earth now, __ join - ing with cre - a - tion, __

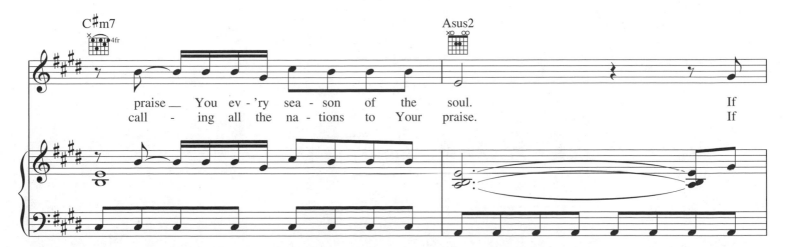

praise __ You ev - 'ry sea - son of the soul. If
call - ing all the na - tions to Your praise. If

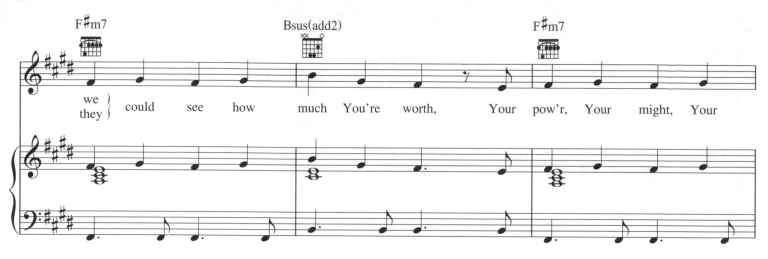

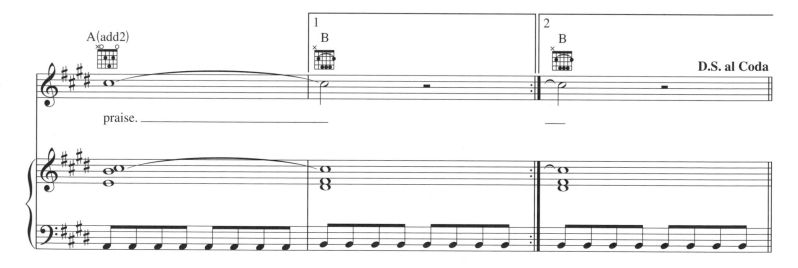

LET MY WORDS BE FEW

(I'll Stand in Awe of You)

Words and Music by MATT REDMAN
and BETH REDMAN

LORD, LET YOUR GLORY FALL

Words and Music by
MATT REDMAN

Moderately slow

You are good, You are good and Your love en-dures.___ You are

good, You are good and Your love en - dures.___ You are good, You are good and Your

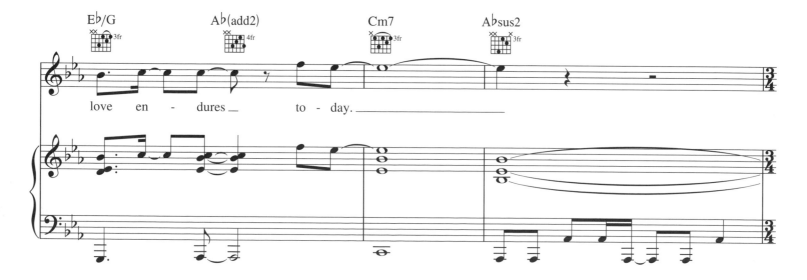

love en - dures ___ to - day. _____

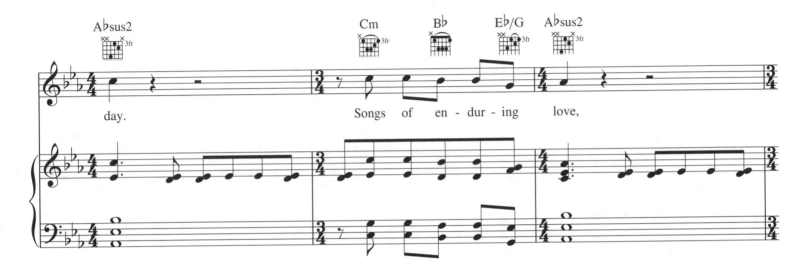

our hearts will sing that song. God, let Your glo - ry

come. You are good, You are good and Your

love en - dures. ___ You are good, You are good and Your

love en - dures. ___ You are good, You are good and Your

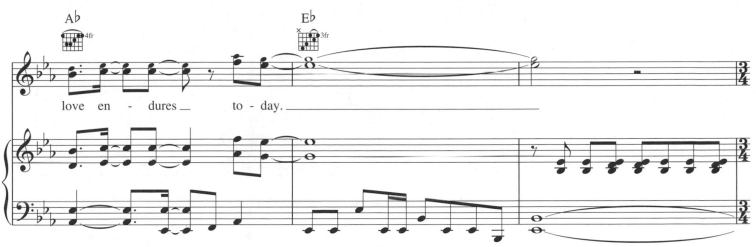

love en - dures __ to - day. _____

Voic - es in u - ni - son   giv - ing You thanks and

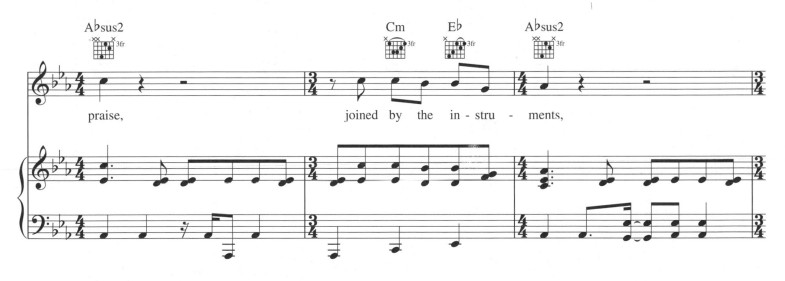

praise,   joined by the in - stru - ments,

and then Your glo - ry came.   Your pres - ence, like a

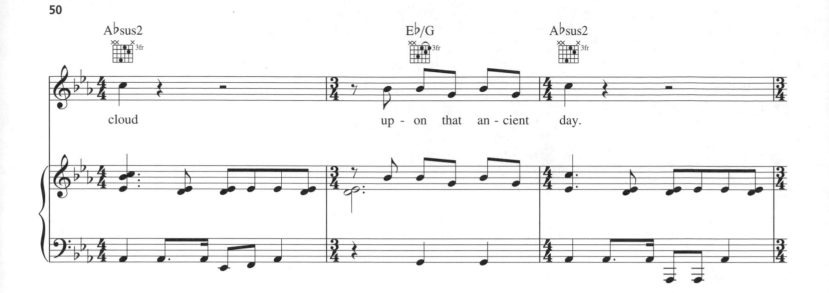

cloud up - on that an - cient day.

The priests were o - ver - whelmed be - cause Your glo - ry

(You are so good.)

came. You are good, You are good and Your

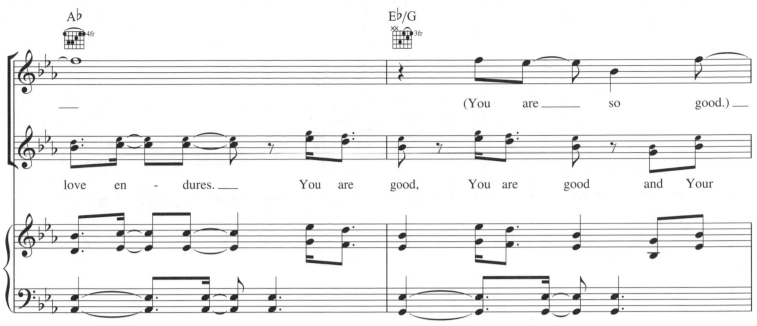

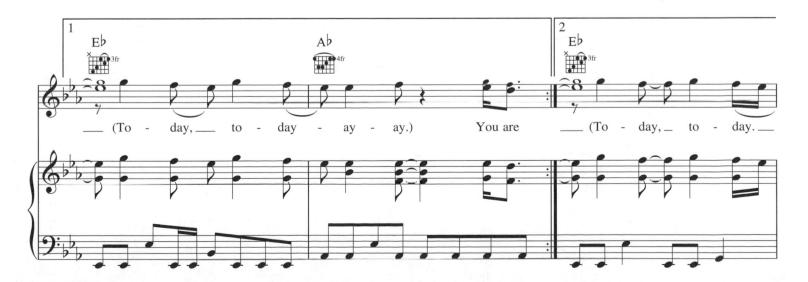

Oh, Your an - ger lasts a mo - ment, but Your

fa - vor lasts a life - time. ___ Your

an - ger lasts__ a mo - ment, but Your fa - vor lasts__ a life - time.

A sac - ri - fice was made,

and then Your fi - re came. They knelt up - on the

ground and with one voice, they praised.

They sang, "Come, Lord. _

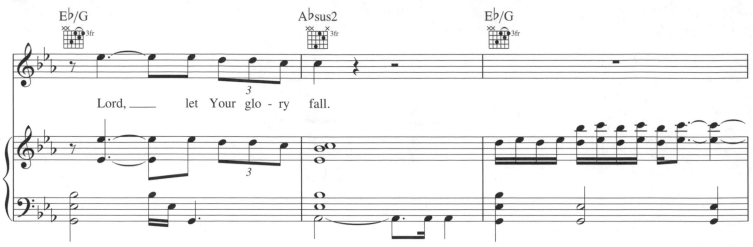

Lord, ___ let Your glo - ry fall.

Let ___ Your glo - ry fall. Come, ___ Lord Je - sus. You are

good, You are good and Your love en - dures. ___ You are

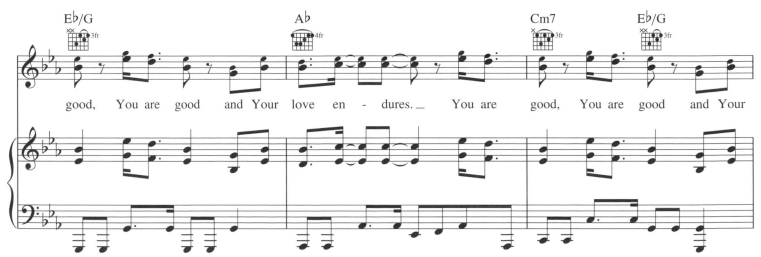

good, You are good and Your love en - dures. ___ You are good, You are good and Your

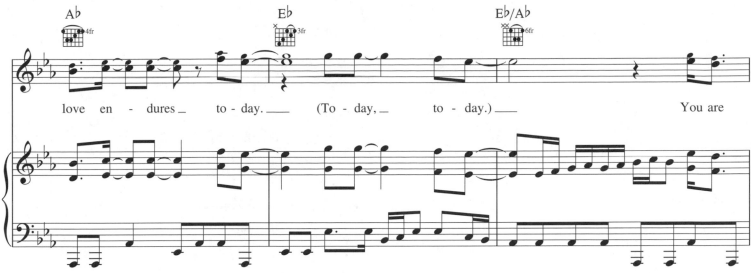

love en - dures _ to - day. _ (To - day, _ to - day.) _ You are

(You are _ so good.) _

good, You are good and Your love en - dures. _ You are

(You are _ so good.) _

good, You are good and Your love en - dures. _ You are

(You are ___ so good.) ___

good, You are good and Your love en - dures ___ to - day. ___

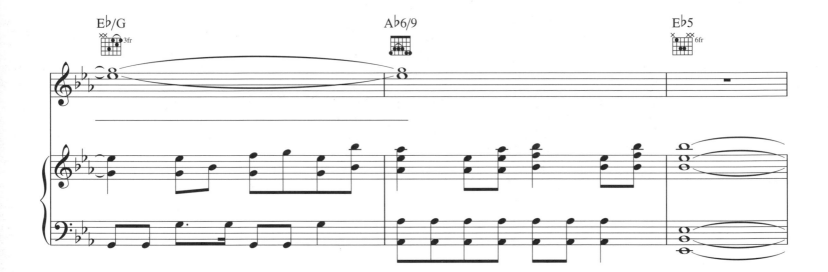

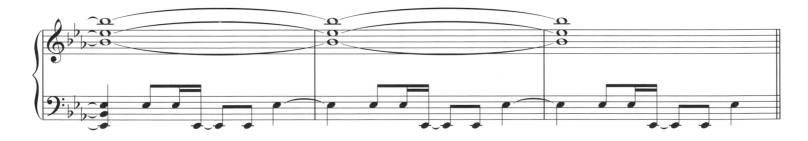

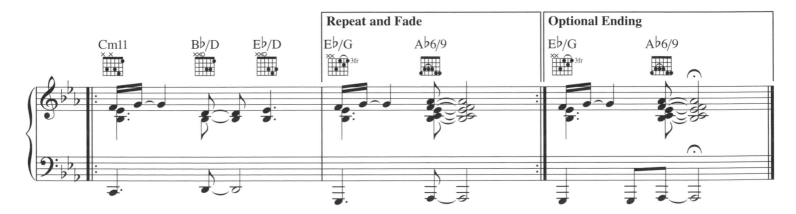

NOTHING BUT THE BLOOD

Words and Music by
MATT REDMAN

Your blood speaks a bet - ter word _

than all the emp - ty claims _ I've heard up - on _ this earth, _

speaks right - eous - ness _ for me, _ it stands in my _ de - fense. _

Recorded a half step lower.

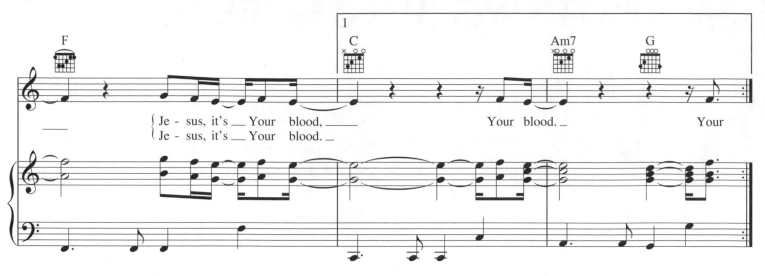

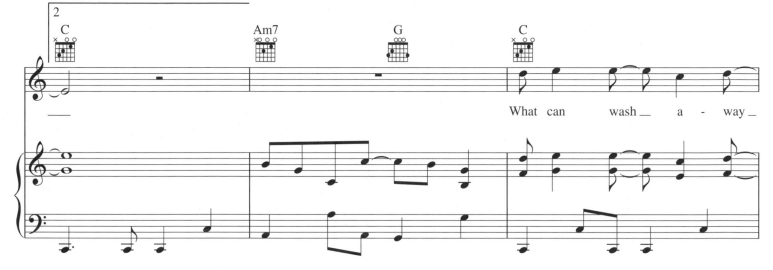

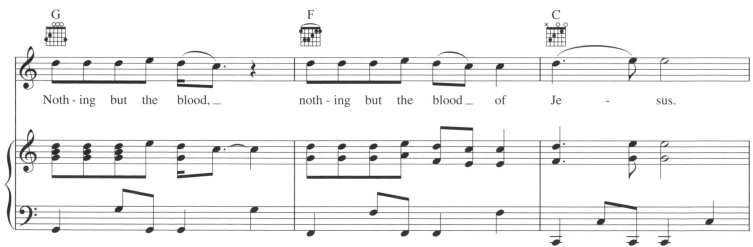

What can wash __ us pure __ as snow, __

wel - comed as __ the friends __ of God? __ Noth - ing but Your blood, __

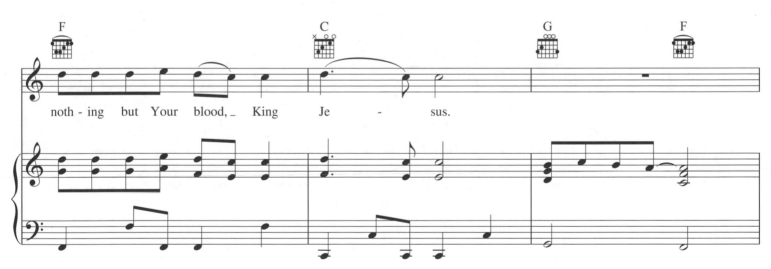

noth - ing but Your blood, __ King Je - sus.

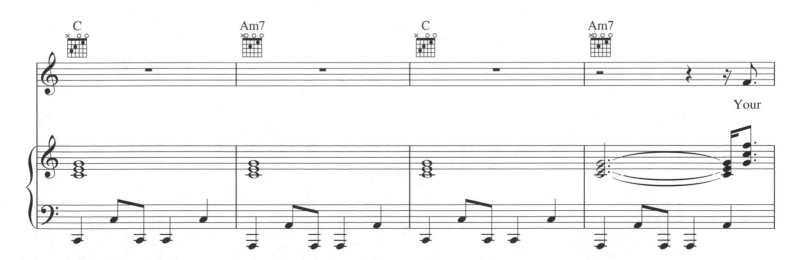

Your

60

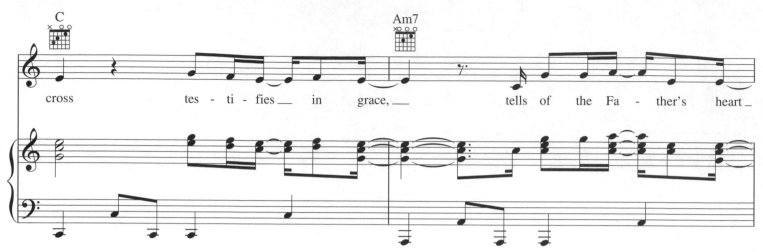

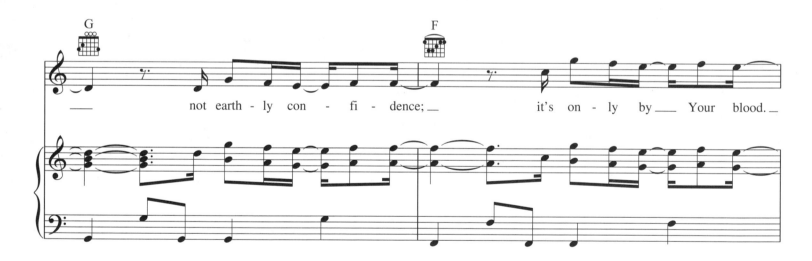

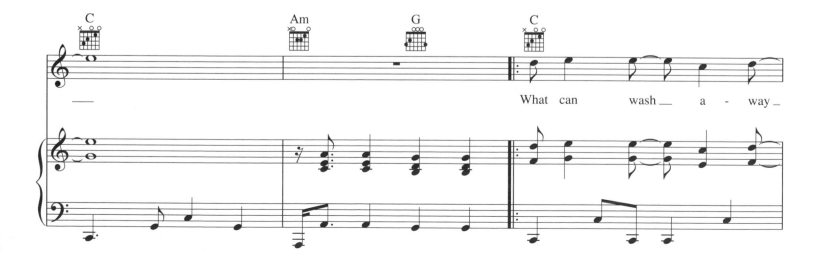

our sins? __ What can make __ us whole __ a - gain? __

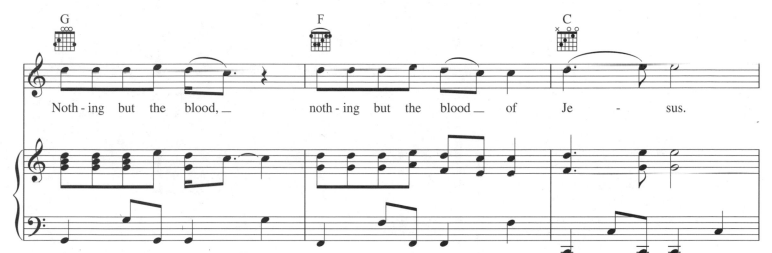

Noth - ing but the blood, __ noth - ing but the blood __ of Je - sus.

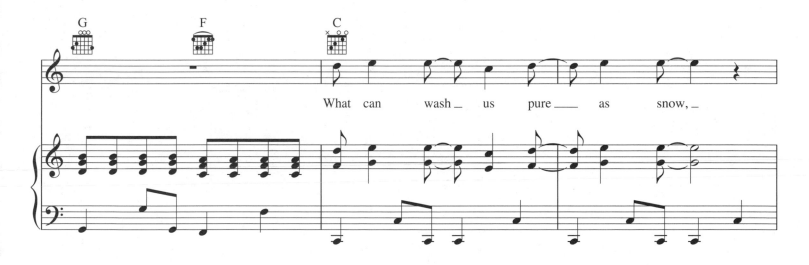

What can wash __ us pure __ as snow, __

wel - comed as __ the friends __ of God? __ Noth - ing but Your blood, __

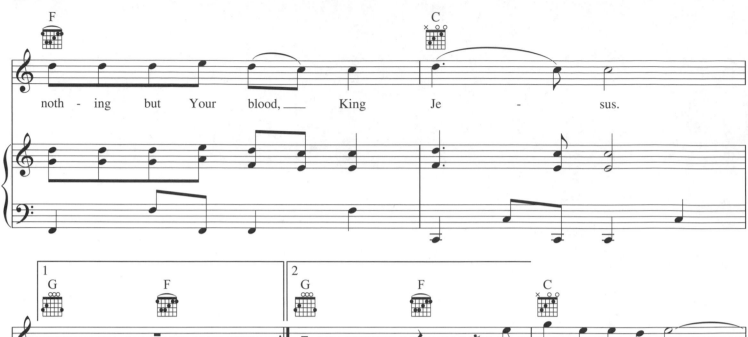

noth - ing but Your blood, ___ King Je - sus.

We praise You for the blood. _____

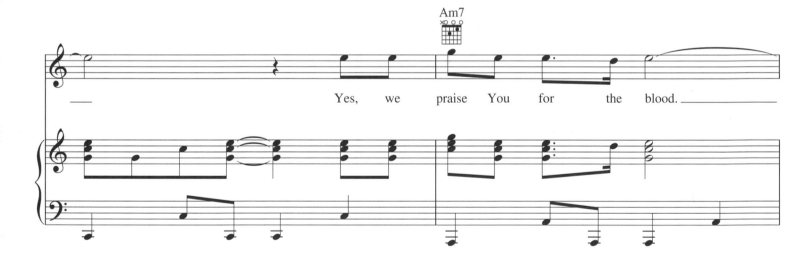

Yes, we praise You for the blood. _____

We've been ran - somed, _ we've been held, we've been re -

SHINE

Words and Music by
MATT REDMAN

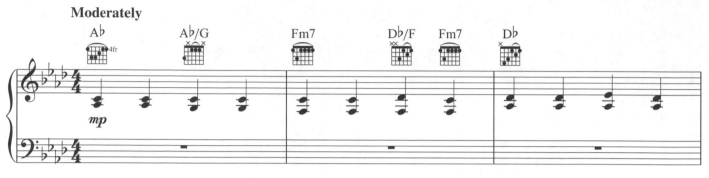

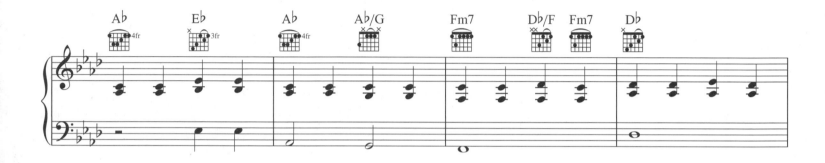

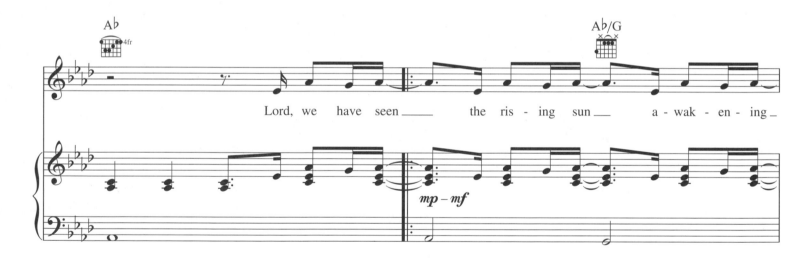

Lord, we have seen ___ the ris - ing sun ___ a - wak - en - ing ___

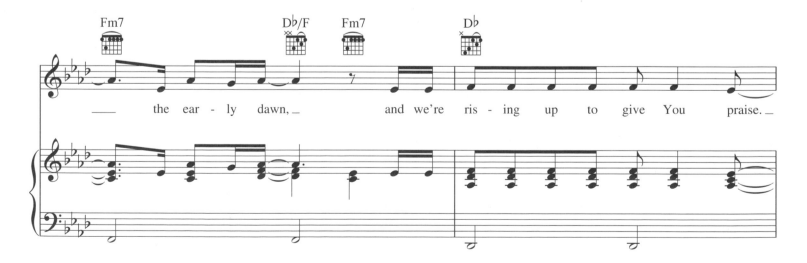

___ the ear - ly dawn, ___ and we're ris - ing up to give You praise. ___

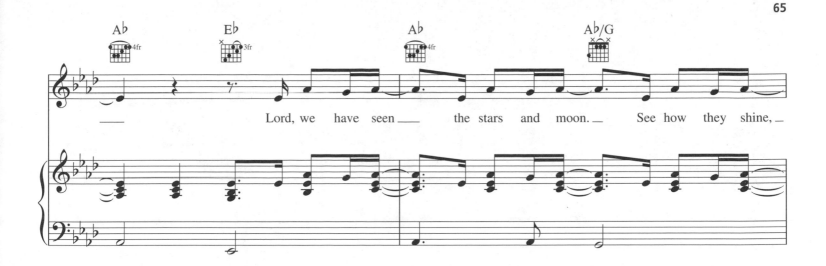

Lord, we have seen ___ the stars and moon. ___ See how they shine, ___

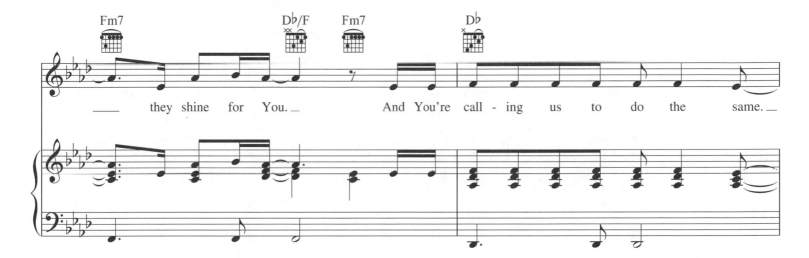

___ they shine for You. ___ And You're call - ing us to do the same. ___

___ So we rise ___ up with a song, ___ and we rise ___

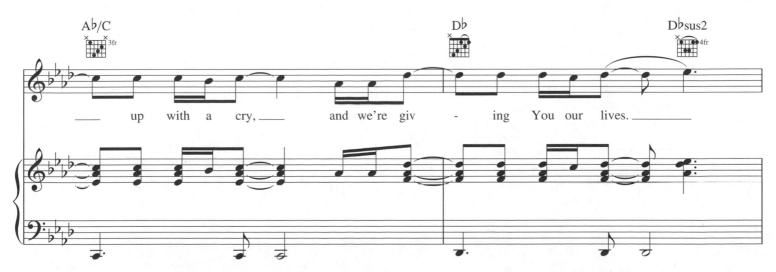

___ up with a cry, ___ and we're giv - ing You our lives. ___

Oh, we will burn so bright with Your praise,

O God, and de - clare Your light to this bro -

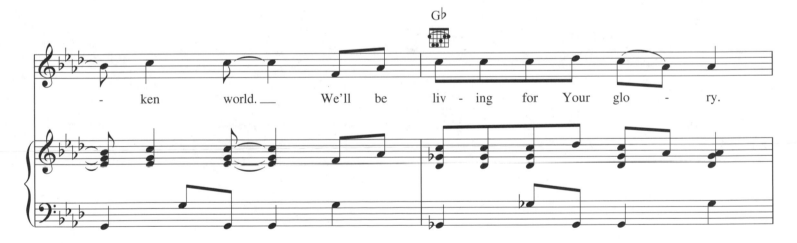

- ken world. We'll be liv - ing for Your glo - ry.

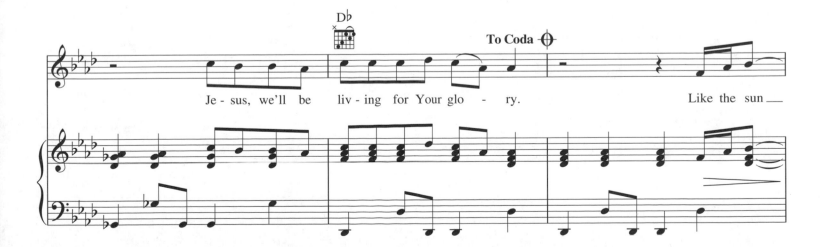

Je - sus, we'll be liv - ing for Your glo - ry. Like the sun

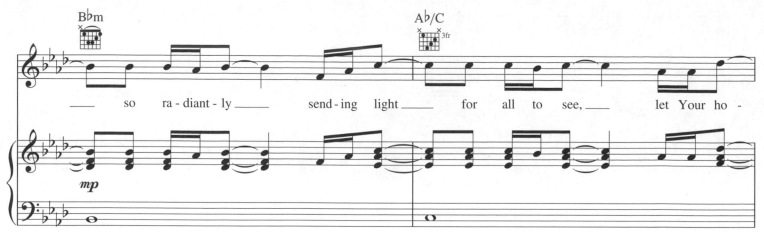

_____ so ra-diant-ly _____ send-ing light _____ for all to see, _____ let Your ho-

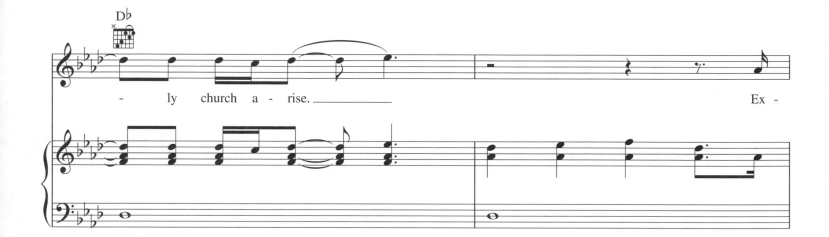

-ly church a - rise. _____ Ex-

plod-ing in-to life, _____ like a su - per-no-va's light, _____ set Your ho-

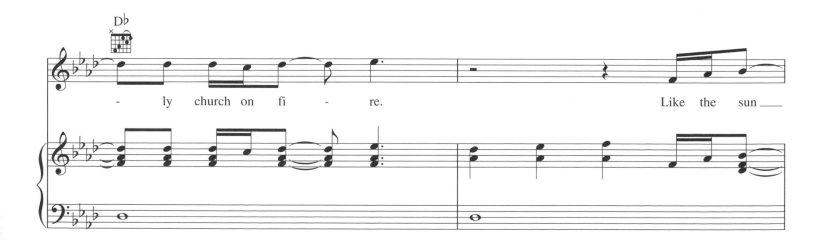

-ly church on fi - re. Like the sun _____

so ra-diant-ly ___ send-ing light ___ for all to see, ___ let Your ho-

-ly church a-rise. ___ Ex-

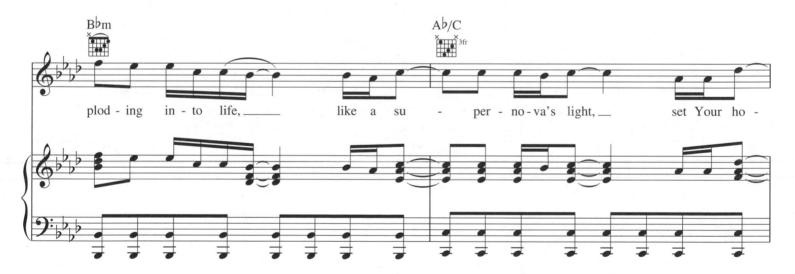

plod-ing in-to life, ___ like a su - per-no-va's light, ___ set Your ho-

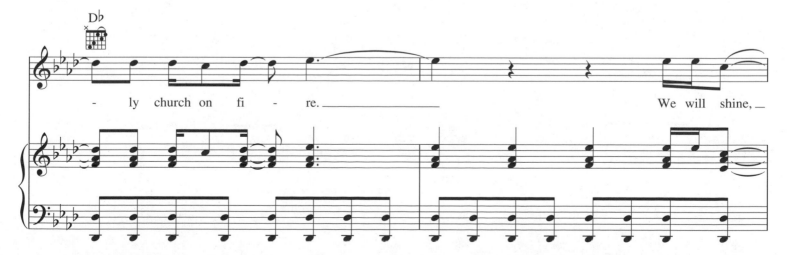

-ly church on fi - re. ___ We will shine, ___

yeah. _____ We will shine. _____

D.S. al Coda
(take 2nd ending)

CODA

_____ We will shine ___

Oh, ___ so we rise ___

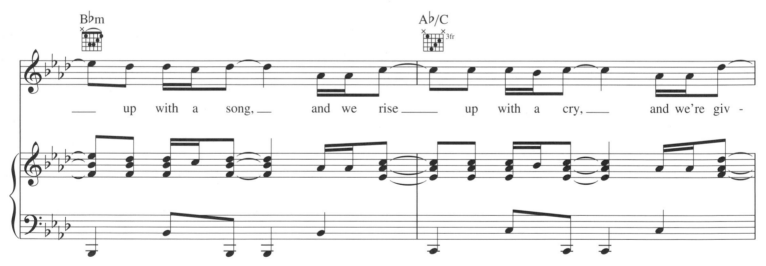

_____ up with a song, ___ and we rise _____ up with a cry, ___ and we're giv -

- ing You our lives. _____

Je - sus, we will shine. _____

ONCE AGAIN

Words and Music by
MATT REDMAN

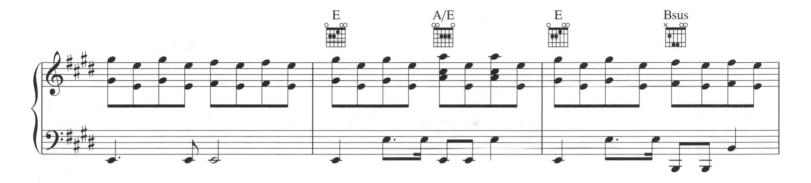

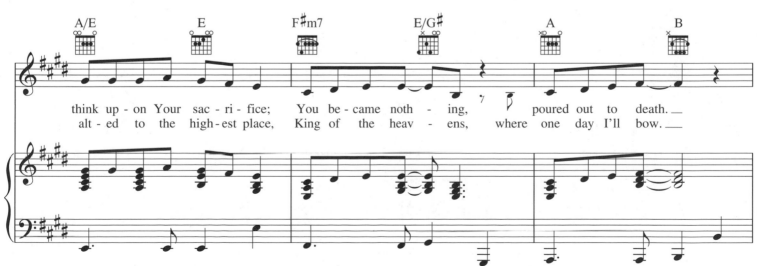

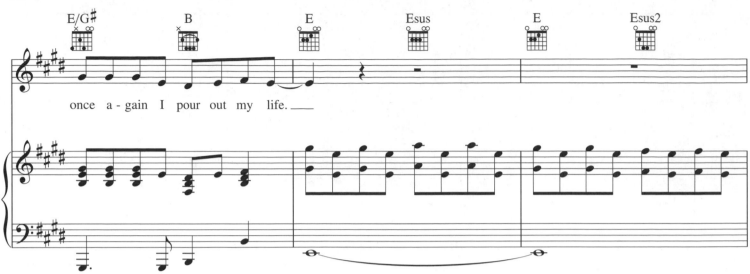

once a-gain I pour out my life. _____

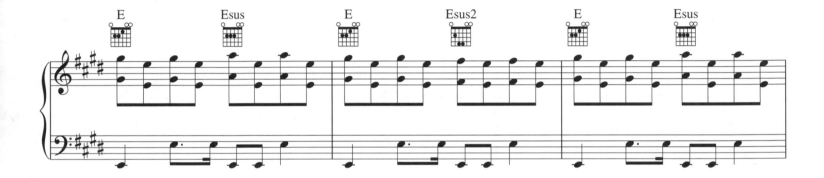

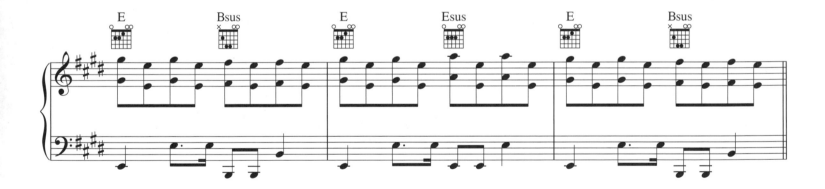

Thank You for the cross,   thank You for the cross,   thank You for the cross, my

Friend.   Thank You for the cross,   thank You for the   cross, ___

thank You for the   cross, my   Friend. ___   Friend.

My   Friend.
(Vocal 1st time only)

UNDIGNIFIED

Words and Music by
MATT REDMAN

Moderately fast

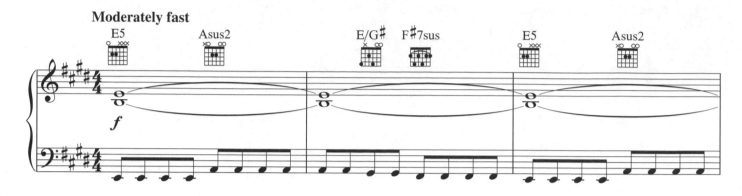

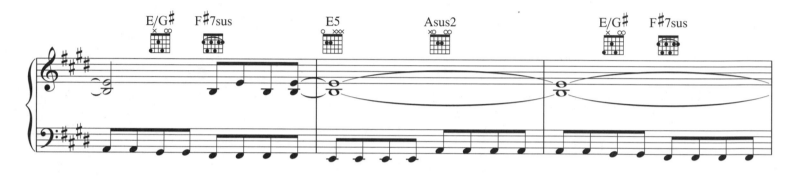

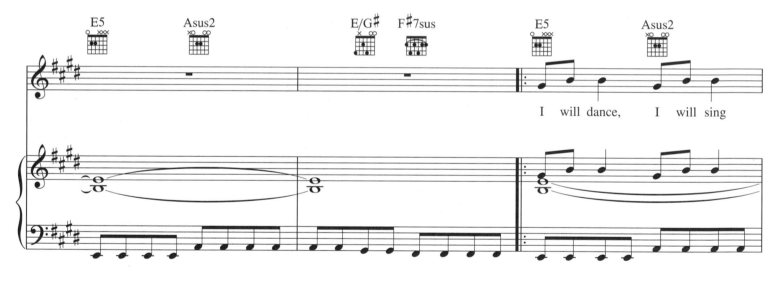

I will dance, I will sing

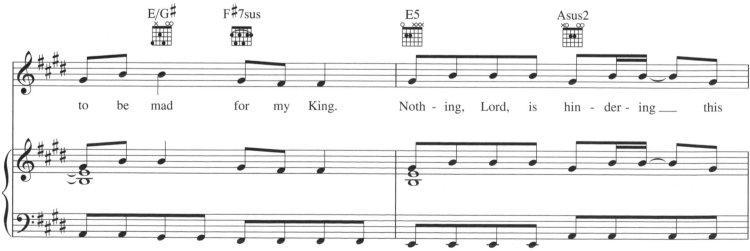

to be mad for my King. Noth-ing, Lord, is hin-der-ing ___ this

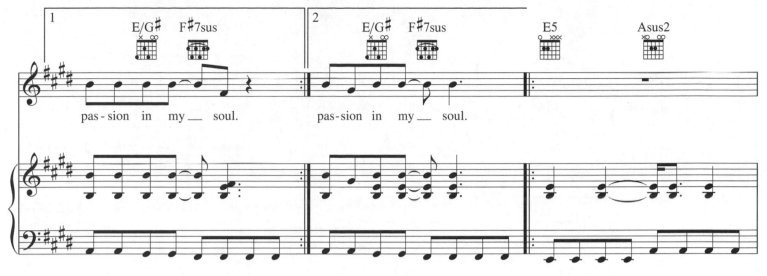

pas-sion in my __ soul.

pas-sion in my __ soul.

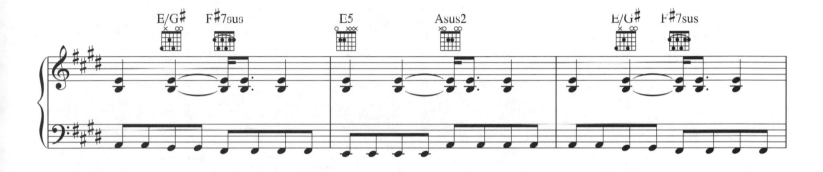

I will dance, I will sing to be mad for my King.

Noth-ing, Lord, is hin-der-ing __ this pas-sion in my __ soul.

80

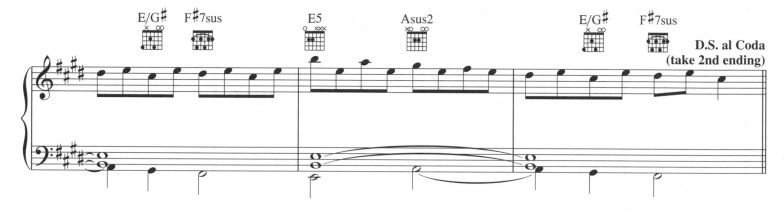

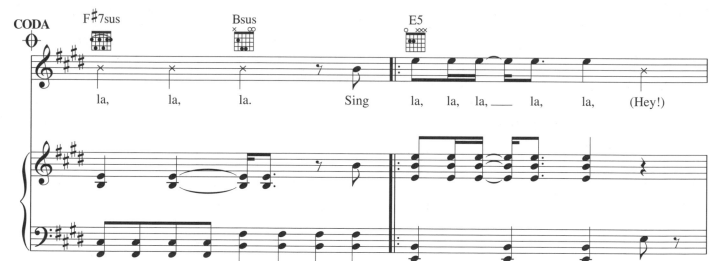

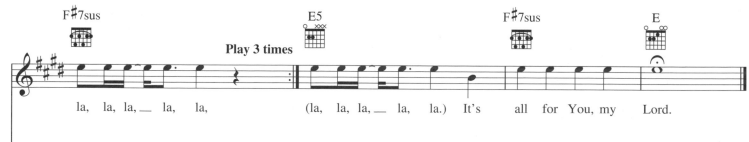

YOU NEVER LET GO

Words and Music by MATT REDMAN
and BETH REDMAN

Recorded a half step lower.

storms of this life, _____ I won't turn back; I know You are near. __
til that day comes, __ we'll live to know You here on the earth. __

__ And I will fear no e -

vil, for my God is with _____

me. And if my God is with _____

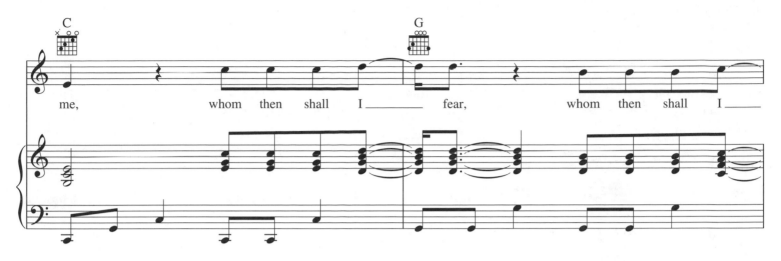

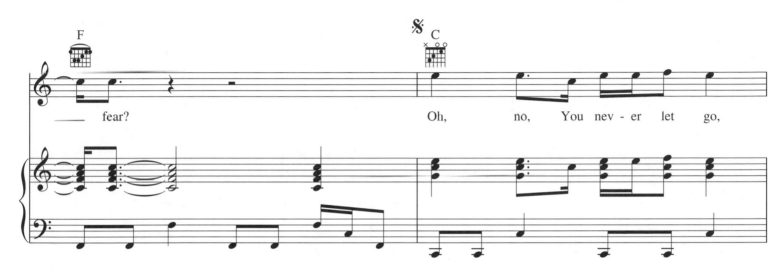

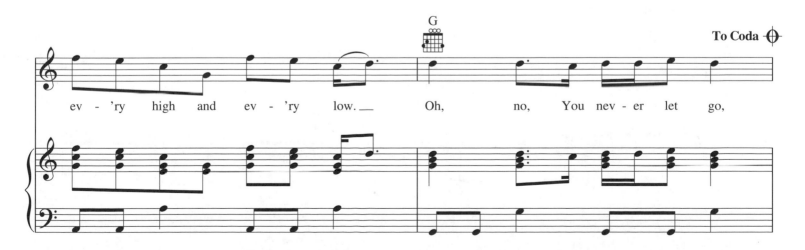

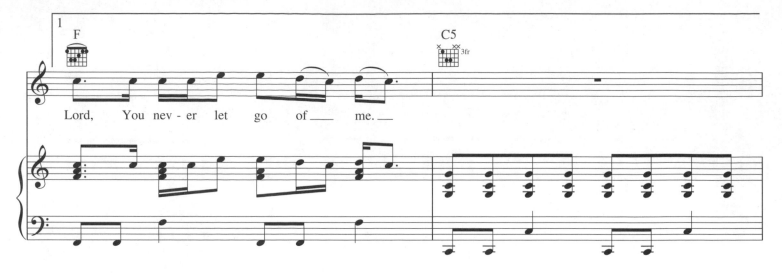

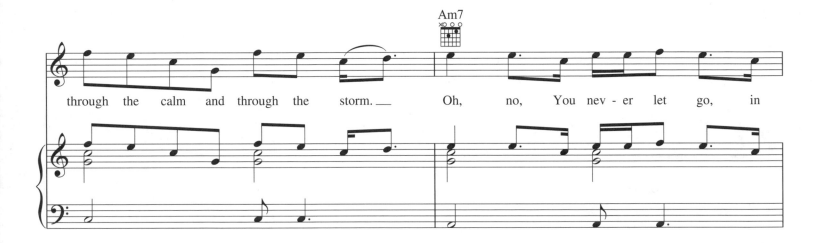

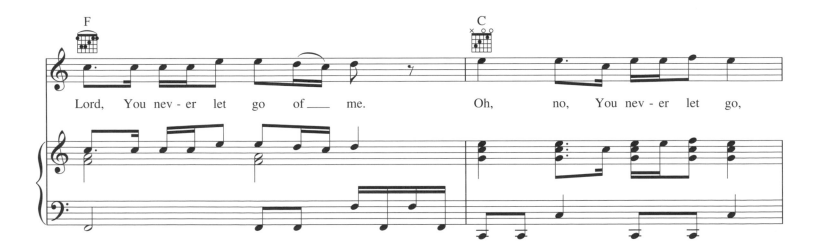

through the calm and through the ___ storm. ___ Oh, no, You nev-er let go, in

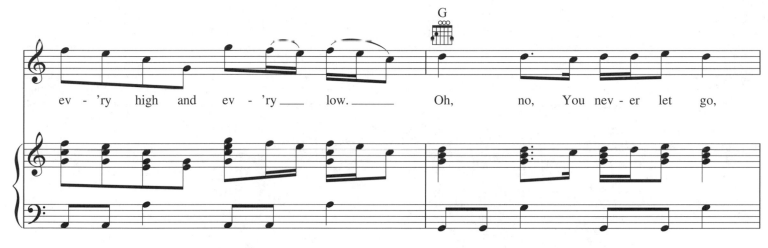

ev-'ry high and ev-'ry ___ low. ___ Oh, no, You nev-er let go,

Lord, You nev-er let go of ___ me. ___

Lord, You nev-er let go of ___ me. ___

More Contemporary Christian Folios from Hal Leonard

Arranged for Piano, Voice and Guitar

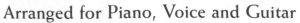

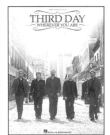
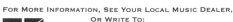